Lifelines 9

Bulwer-Lytton
*An illustrated life of the first
Baron Lytton*

1803-1873
Sibylla Jane Flower

Shire Publications Ltd.

Contents

ACKNOWLEDGEMENTS

The author and publishers wish to thank the following for permission to reproduce the illustrations on the pages indicated: the Garrick Club 27 (lower); English Life Publications Ltd. 9 (right), 12; National Portrait Gallery 23 (lower), 35 (right); Victoria and Albert Museum 17, 18. The cover design by Roger Fuller features a cartoon of Bulwer-Lytton by 'Ape'.

Printed by Maund and Irvine Ltd., Tring, Herts.

Opposite: Edward Bulwer-Lytton at Knebworth by Thomas Macquoid R.A., 1872 (figure by Leslie Ward, 'Spy').

Lord Lytton
Sketched from memo.
Knebworth
E M Ward RA
Aug. 18th 1817

Early years

Edward George Earle Lytton Bulwer was born on 25th May 1803 at 31 Baker Street, London. He was the son of a general, a strong-willed, ambitious and gout-ridden man who died in 1807. Thus he can have remembered little of his father; certainly not enough to justify the scorn with which he referred to him in his autobiography, a view derived presumably from his mother, whose prejudice against her husband softened little in the long years of her widowhood. To Elizabeth Bulwer-Lytton, Edward was a godsend; her eldest son, William, succeeded to the Bulwer estates and the second, Henry, was adopted by his maternal grandmother. Edward was her favourite, and upon him she lavished love, guidance and her own somewhat depleted inheritance, which effectively meant her father's debts and the large, rambling, Tudor house at Knebworth.

Bulwer's* education was erratic; various schools took his mother's fancy; Dr Hooker's at Rottingdean was one, where Bulwer so distinguished himself that he persuaded her that it was pointless to send him to Eton, and Mr Wallington's at Ealing another, where Bulwer was encouraged to publish his first collection of poems.

In later life Bulwer always referred to the most important incident of his childhood as the arrival in 1810 of his grandfather Richard Warburton Lytton's library. The books had to be sold eventually to defray the old scholar's debts but for a year they remained at Mrs Bulwer-Lytton's house in

*So he will be referred to, for convenience sake, in this book. He was christened Edward George Earle Lytton Bulwer. In 1838 he was created Sir Edward Lytton Bulwer, Bart. On the death of his mother in 1843 he assumed the additional name of Lytton, hyphenated as 'Bulwer-Lytton'. He was raised to the peerage as the 1st Baron Lytton in 1866.

Opposite: Edward Bulwer-Lytton sketched from memory by E.M.Ward R.A., 18th August 1869.

Nottingham Place. 'I was Solomon in all his glory,' Bulwer recalled, 'and surrounded by all his seraglio.'

Although the Bulwers had been established in Norfolk for generations, it was the Lytton family who were to prove of almost obsessive interest to Bulwer. The pride he felt in this branch of his family and its endless ramifications he considered a formative influence on his early passion for history; his Tudor descent is the theme of the decoration of his drawing room at Knebworth and the forty-four quarterings of his mother are depicted on the ceiling and around the frieze.

FIRST LOVES

At Ealing, Bulwer fell in love with a girl who was forced by her father to marry another man. Three years later she died, but not before she had reaffirmed her love for Bulwer, a love which he remembered with bitter regret all his life. He visited her grave at Ullswater in 1824 and in *Kenelm Chillingly*, a book he finished a few days before his death, he drew her lovingly as Lily Mordaunt.

Bulwer went up to Cambridge with thoughts of nothing but his lost love. The first days were miserable and he loathed Trinity College. In 1822 he became a Fellow Commoner of Trinity Hall and was much happier. He joined the Union Debating Society at the prompting of his new-found friend Alexander Cockburn, later Lord ~~Chancellor~~, and here he heard Macaulay speak and learned much of the art of debate. He read copiously and laid the foundations of his wide-ranging studies. In 1825 he won the Chancellor's Gold Medal for his poem 'Sculpture'.

In his last year at Cambridge Bulwer fell under the spell of Lady Caroline Lamb whose home at Brocket was a short ride from Knebworth. It was unfortunate; the affair was brief, but Bulwer suffered greatly at her hands. They remained friends, however, and she was a constant source of support to him in his early literary life; she introduced him to William Godwin and at her death she left him her miniature of Byron.

After Cambridge, Bulwer spent some time travelling on the continent. He was in Paris for much of the winter of 1825 enjoying the social life to the full and retreating from time to time to Versailles to read and study in peace. Much of his first taste of fashionable Parisian life is reflected in the pages of

ISMAEL;

AN ORIENTAL TALE.

WITH

Other Poems.

BY

EDWARD GEORGE LYTTON BULWER.

Written between
The Age of Thirteen and Fifteen.

" Scribimus indocti doctique poëmata passim."
Hor. 2 *Ep.* 1.

LONDON:

PRINTED FOR J. HATCHARD AND SON,
No. 187, PICCADILLY.

1820.

Frontispiece of 'Ismael', containing poems written by Bulwer as a boy, 1820.

7

Pelham, which was gradually taking shape in his mind.

In Paris he met an Englishwoman, Mrs Cunningham, who sympathised with him, understood him and was able to provide him with that lively, intelligent companionship he had so appreciated in Lady Caroline Lamb but without the romantic snare into which Caroline had drawn him. It is through the eyes of Mrs Cunningham's daughter that Bulwer is first glimpsed, aged twenty-two, 'old and wise' to the notions of a fifteen-year-old girl, with a distinctive form of dress and 'beautiful curls'.

MARRIAGE TO ROSINA

In April 1826 he returned to London. The Fates, who stalked Bulwer throughout his life in female form, awaited him. He had been back a matter of hours when he met at a party the woman to whom he was to be bound in love and in hatred for the rest of his life, Rosina Doyle Wheeler. Rosina was twenty-four, the offspring of a penniless, wretchedly unhappy family of good birth but scant breeding from County Limerick. She was a girl of striking beauty, lively, amusing and ambitious; she was also a protegée of Lady Caroline Lamb. Rosina never forgot her first glimpse of Bulwer and the giggle which she and Letitia Landon stifled as they caught sight of him as he entered the drawing room with his mother: his golden hair hanging in ringlets almost to his shoulders, his 'fairy-like lingerie', the three inches of cambric encircling his coat cuffs, and the ebony cane which dangled with studied precision from his hand, a-glitter with rings. But Rosina was flattered by his attentions. The favourite son of an apparently rich widow, the winner of the Chancellor's prize, looks, fortune, fame; it needed only the prompting of Caroline Lamb to have them, within a matter of weeks, in each other's arms at Brocket. Bulwer wrote to Rosina, 'I touched you, I held your hand in mine, and I felt as if you alone were all the world. What were Reason, Resolution, the wisdom of Premeditation, to the impulse of that unguarded instant.'

On 29th August 1827, after a stormy engagement, Bulwer and Rosina were married at St James's, Piccadilly. Mrs Bulwer-Lytton, upon whom Bulwer was wholly dependent financially, strongly disapproved of the match, refused to receive her daughter-in-law and, most tragically for her son's literary career, stopped his allowance. They settled happily at

*Above: Rosina Doyle Wheeler,
who married Bulwer in 1827.*

*Edward Bulwer-Lytton by Daniel
Maclise, 1850.*

9

first at Woodcot, near Pangbourne on the Thames, and there in July 1829 their first child Emily was born. But it was an isolated house, Bulwer was obliged to make frequent visits to London and when he was at home he had little time to spare for Rosina. For Bulwer it was a life of literary drudgery; all his life he recalled with bitterness the early years of hack writing for periodicals, 'the grave of much genius', as he wrote with feeling in the obituary of his friend Laman Blanchard. During the ten years between his marriage and the final separation from his wife, Bulwer completed ten novels, two long poems, a play, and numerous contributions to the journals of the day; for a time he was editor of a literary magazine and after his election in 1831 he had in addition his parliamentary duties. The effort told both upon his health and his temper; Rosina's loneliness increased. In January 1830 they moved to London, to 36 Hertford Street where they entertained lavishly; in 1831, their second child Robert was born.

London life was some consolation to Rosina but the neglect she suffered at her husband's hands proved increasingly galling. Superficially, the days appeared golden. The Bulwers planned their assault on London life with meticulous care; before long, invitations to 36 Hertford Street were eagerly sought after. The young Disraeli, who had much in common with Bulwer, wrote to his sister after one glittering dinner: 'Our host, whatever may be his situation, was more sumptuous and fantastic than ever. Mrs Bulwer was a blaze of jewels and looked like Juno; only instead of a peacock she had a dog in her lap called Fairy.'

Bookmark worked by Emily for her father.

Early literary life

BULWER AS JOURNALIST

It is easy to forget the degree to which politics invaded every branch of journalism at the time Bulwer began his literary career. An author could hope for nothing from an editor whose political views did not coincide with his own; as for the literary magazines which belonged to the most powerful publishing houses, justice to a rival's protegé was virtually unknown. Bulwer's early connection with the *Westminster Review* and his liberal sympathies aroused the instant suspicions of the Tory Press and his first publisher, Henry Colburn, who had enraged his colleagues by his radical attitude to publishing, was another connection frowned upon by conservatives. Thus the niche Bulwer chose for himself was controversial from the start.

It was, however, in the pages of a lesser magazine than the *Westminster* that Bulwer began his journalistic career. In 1823 a group of distinguished Cambridge men persuaded the publisher Charles Knight to launch a quarterly on the lines of *Blackwood.* Bulwer made several contributions to *Knight's Quarterly Magazine* in the years 1823 and 1824 under the pseudonym Edmund Bruce. His introduction to the magazine's readers was written by Winthrop Mackworth Praed; it was prophetic. 'I have a friend who writes more verses than any man under the sun. I will engage that he shall spill more ink in an hour than a County Member shall swallow claret.'

By 1828 Bulwer had had his first clash with the critics; the poem 'Sculpture' which had won him the Chancellor's Gold Medal was seized upon by *Fraser's Magazine* and held up to ridicule. Bulwer reacted sharply, as he was to do all his life. He wrote feelingly of the perils of authorship in *Maltravers* as a surrender of a name 'to men's tongues', something to which he could never reconcile himself. In the case of *Fraser's Magazine* this was fair enough, for he was pursued in its pages with

'Little Boots', Bulwer's daughter Emily, by Daniel Maclise.

dedicated venom throughout the 1830s. 'Bulwer-baiting', as Michael Sadleir wrote, began as an automatic joke and developed into the accepted sport of a small but vociferous group of intellectuals. Much in Bulwer's work invited hostility; and his manner (described by Samuel Carter Hall as 'that aristocratic something bordering on hauteur'), his dress, his affectations and his ostentatious way of life, provided ammunition for a war which was waged against him as much personally as it was professionally.

THE FIRST NOVELS

The novel which Bulwer submitted to Colburn in the autumn of that year was at first rejected by the publisher's reader. Colburn, when urged to read it, had no doubts. *Pelham or the Adventures of a Gentleman* appeared on 10th March 1828; the book's authorship was a closely guarded secret. At first it hung fire but after two months it began to sell; it became the book of the year. To present-day readers it is easily the most enjoyable of all Bulwer's works. A delightful satire, witty and urbane, on the fashionable world of London and Paris in the 1820s, the pages sparkle with a gaiety and humour which rarely reappear in Bulwer's later works. The characters are unforgettable: Pelham himself, who lent his name to describe any young buck about town, whose black coat instantly banished the usual plum or blue from evening parties virtually to this day, and who was described by his creator as fop and philosopher, voluptuary and moralist; John Russelton, 'who had introduced, by a single example, starch into neckcloths, and had fed the pampered appetite of his boot-tops on champagne'; Mr Wormwood, 'the *noli-me-tangere* of literary lions'; Sir Lionel Garrett, 'pinched in, and curled out'; and Pelham's old friend of Cambridge days, the Reverend Christopher Clutterbuck, in whose house he was offered 'a towel, of so coarse a huckaback, that I did not dare adventure its rough texture next my complexion'.

Pelham established the author's literary reputation; the satire was not lost on the press of left or right; the radical *Examiner's* review was favourable, for they had sensed with glee the scorn which lay beneath the polished prose.

The two next novels, *The Disowned* (1828) and *Devereux* (1829), were very different in character. The *Examiner* quipped that Bulwer had written *Pelham* for pleasure, *The Disowned* for

Lady Blessington conducted a brilliant salon at Gore House, Kensington, where she moved in 1836. Her 'Journal of Conversations with Lord Byron' created a sensation when published by Bulwer in the 'New Monthly Magazine', 1832-3.

the bookseller and *Devereux* for his public, and there was some truth in this. He received £800 for the copyright of *The Disowned* and though the book had an enormous success in its day, it is tedious to a modern reader. Those who had seen great promise in *Pelham* were sadly disappointed. *Devereux* was set in the early eighteenth century and, though it was written in haste with Colburn's handsome offer of £1,500 in mind, much extensive reading and study of the reign of Queen Anne went into its preparation. The book failed dismally and later Bulwer freely admitted that it was among the least successful of all his writings.

As the need for money became more pressing, so Bulwer worked at greater speed. These were still relatively peaceful days at home and in the researches for the next novel, *Paul Clifford,* which followed quickly on the heels of *Devereux,* Rosina assisted by helping with notes from the *Newgate Calendar. Paul Clifford* was the first of his reforming works, written with the avowed purpose of placing before the public some of the iniquities of the penal code and the prison system. Many of the worst excesses were swept away in the Reform Parliament of 1832, in which Bulwer played his part to the full, but a measure of the strength of his feelings before reform can be gauged from the pages of *Paul Clifford.* The hero of the novel was a highwayman, a matter of some surprise to an early nineteenth-century reader, but he was also a gentleman highwayman, which was not only surprising but also rather shocking. The book was a great success despite the high moral tone of some of the critics. It can still be read with pleasure by a modern reader despite the verbosity which had become by this date a feature of Bulwer's style.

LONDON AND LADY BLESSINGTON

The year 1831 was spent in even more unremitting labour. The move to Hertford Steet had taken place and in April he had entered the House of Commons as member for St Ives. Bulwer was forging friendships not only in the world of fashion but also, and increasingly so, with writers, journalists and politicians. In the autumn he met Lady Blessington and instantly became absorbed into her brilliant circle; Disraeli was already a close friend and the year before had sent the manuscript of *The Young Duke* for Bulwer's comments. Bulwer was 'one of the few with whom my intellect comes into collision with benefit', Disraeli wrote in his diary in 1833.

In November, Bulwer took over the editorship of the *New Monthly Magazine* from Thomas Campbell; it was journalism, but it was money, and again it meant new contacts, new friends. Not all Bulwer's acquaintances were acceptable to Rosina by any means. Samuel Carter Hall, Bulwer's deputy editor, called one day at Hertford Street. The evening before Bulwer had entertained to dinner Daniel O'Connell and some of the other Irish M.Ps. Hall found Rosina in the dining room which 'she was *fumigating* in order to get rid of the brogue'.

In January 1832 *Eugene Aram* was published. The story of the scholar-murderer and his life during the fourteen years between the crime, his arrest and his sensational trial was fresh in the minds of most of Bulwer's readers. Strangely, Bulwer chose to deviate from the known facts. John Forster voiced the opinion of many of the book's critics when he confessed that although he had read the book with 'very great and greedy pleasure', he wished that Bulwer had followed more carefully the few facts that were known of the nature of the crime. But the book was a huge success with the public. The Gothic romance of *Godolphin* which formed a pendant to *Eugene Aram* appeared anonymously in April 1833 and bears, unmistakably, the signs of Bulwer's mental stress. Parliament, the magazine, the compilation of the remarkably perceptive commentary on *England and the English* which appeared the same year, the vicious attacks of his dedicated enemies at *Fraser's Magazine,* his half-acceptance of the fact that his marriage was doomed, crowded together upon Bulwer's head. He was just thirty. How he survived these days is impossible to tell. 'God gave us imagination and faith, as the two sole instincts of the future,' he wrote in *Zanoni*; faith must somehow have saved him from total despair, for it would have needed a great stretch of the imagination to see an escape from the *impasse* his life had reached. Faith, in Bulwer's own words, was 'the moonlight that sways the tides of the human sea'.

NAPLES AND POMPEII

In September 1833 Rosina and Bulwer set out for Italy, wintering in Naples and returning in the following April. The second honeymoon which had been vaguely envisaged before they set out never materialised; they were miserable together. For Bulwer, in other directions, it was a period of renewal and refreshment. He recovered his health and shattered spirit. The history of Rome became a subject of absorbing interest and it was in Italy that he laid the foundations of the research that went into the writing of *Rienzi*. But his visit to Naples was to prove most stimulating; '. . . beautiful, enchanting, delicious Naples, the only city in all Italy which is quite to my heart,' he

John Forster, close friend of Bulwer and biographer of Dickens, sketched by Daniel Maclise in 1840.

wrote to Lady Blessington—a paradise, in fact, except for the mosquitoes: 'they are worse than a bad conscience, and never let me sleep at nights.' Lady Blessington provided a host of introductions. From Bulwer's point of view the most valuable was his meeting with Sir William Gell whose researches at Pompeii had established his name in archaeological circles. Bulwer spent much time in his company and Gell reported to Lady Blessington that the Bulwers' visit had been a great success and, furthermore, that they had succeeded in coping with the macaroni most creditably. When Bulwer returned to England in the spring of 1834 he brought with him half the manuscript of *Rienzi* and, three-quarters finished. *The Last Days of Pompeii.*

The Last Days of Pompeii is the most abidingly popular of Bulwer's works and the one with which his name is indelibly linked. Bulwer had seen a painting of the destruction of the city in the Brera in Milan on the journey south and the drama and pathos of the scene had impressed themselves on his memory.

When he visited Pompeii, well-furnished by Sir William Gell with stories of the catastrophe, his imagination ran wild, repeopling the streets annihilated seventeen centuries before, the forum, the Roman baths, the Temple of Isis; recreating too, in his mind's eye, the fatal earthquake, the layers of cinder and the molten lava which enveloped the city leaving it dead and the people solidified in the very act of escaping, until the

Bulwer with his pipe, sketched by Daniel Maclise in the early 1830s.

excavations in the eighteenth century uncovered them once more.

The characters in the book are vividly portrayed: Sallust the epicure, Arbaces the Egyptian sorcerer whose smile seemed 'to sadden the very sun', Calenus the priest of the Temple of Isis, the Greek Glaucus who loved the beautiful Ione, Diomed the rich merchant and his daughter Julia, and blind Nydia the flower-seller, the most sympathetic of all Bulwer's female characters, who alone was able to find her way through the darkened streets to safety. The skulls of Arbaces and Calenus had been unearthed at Pompeii in the early nineteenth century and were presented to Bulwer in 1859.

The Last Days of Pompeii was published in July 1834; its

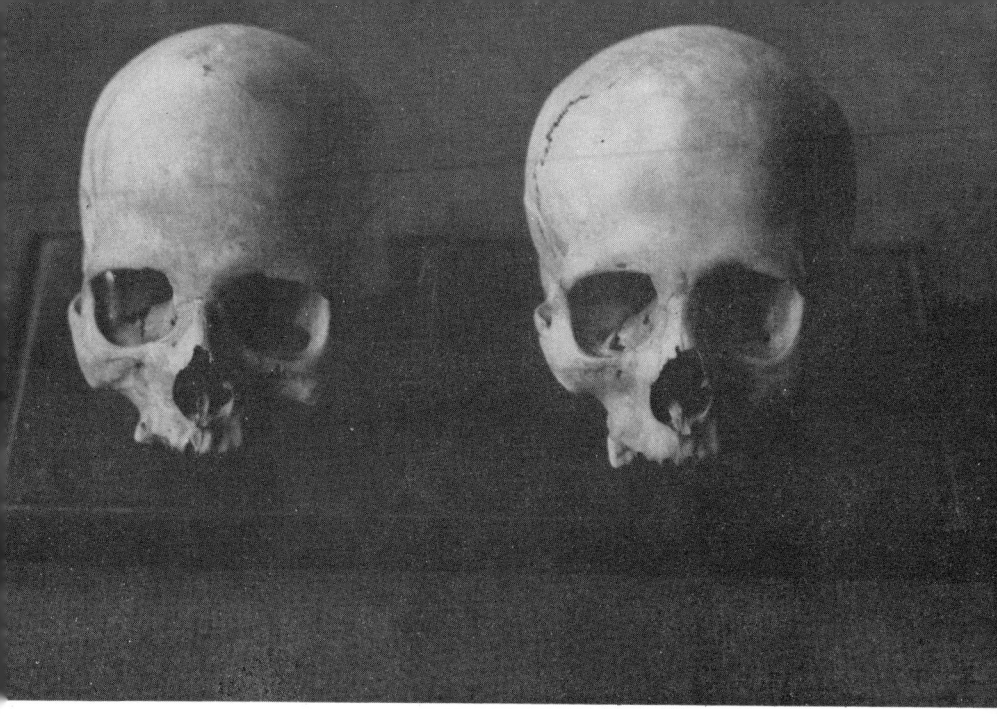

The skulls of Arbaces and Calenus, excavated at Pompeii and given to Bulwer in 1859.

success was immediate and as a work of historical fiction it has had few equals before or since.

In the character of Cola di Rienzi Bulwer found a dazzling and romantic hero. Rienzi was a man of humble birth who rose by sheer ability to supreme power in Rome in 1347. Bulwer was able to paint the picture of a man who combined all the knightly qualities of the fourteenth century with the political principles of the nineteenth-century reformers. The book appeared in December 1835 and remained one of the most popular of all Bulwer's books in his lifetime.

FAME AND SEPARATION

Bulwer's confidence returned; the success of *Pompeii* and *Rienzi* established him in the forefront of contemporary novelists; his acute financial problems were solved; there· was much to be done in Parliament and, although he always spoke from a carefully prepared script, speech-making became gradually less of an ordeal. The shyness concealed by excessive flippancy which so irritated his acquaintances melted in the presence of friends; he was a delightful companion, much in demand socially. The American journalist Nathaniel Parker Willis described Bulwer at a party of Lady Blessington's: 'Gay, quick, various, half-satirical . . . he seemed to talk because he could not help it, and infected everybody with his spirits . . . his clear laugh is the soul of sincere and careless merriment.' Above all, he was known for his generosity whether it was of time or money, both precious to him, or of advice, and many struggling authors were grateful for his concern. It must have come as a surprise to many to find that the dandified author, haughty and proud, was also such an immensely human individual. When Lady Holland dared to ask him if the young Charles Dickens was 'presentable', he, in his own words, 'growled and snapped'. As for his elaborate dress, he wrote: 'God gave my soul an exterior abode, and the very fact that there is a soul within the shell, makes me think the shell not to be neglected.' 'A thoroughly satin character,' wrote H.F.Chorley, 'but then it is the richest satin.'

But there was one thorn in Bulwer's flesh, Rosina. The journey to Italy had proved disastrous; the return to England was blighted by passionate accusations of infidelity on both sides. Meetings, separations, quarrels and reconciliations continued until any form of contact between them became agonising. In April 1836 a deed of separation was signed. Sadly, that was not the end of the story; the unhappy saga continued. Bulwer's life from then on was lived in the limelight of the political stage, the literary front pages or even the boards of Covent Garden itself. Rosina was completely ignored. She had her dogs, occasionally her children, and her solitude, and in this dangerous limbo beneath the fashionable world she craved, she evolved scheme upon scheme to malign and embarrass her husband. Bulwer, the man she had loved, whose every weakness and every fear was at her mercy, was an easy quarry for her wiles, and she pursued him with relentless and savage fury until his death.

The House of Commons

The publication of *Rienzi* at the end of 1835 marks a convenient pause in which to glance at the parliamentary world in which Bulwer had moved since his election in 1831. Throughout his life politics and literature vied for first call on his time and energy. Immersed in politics he longed for literature and the peace to pursue his researches; in the quiet of his study he yearned for the parliamentary stage. He was never to reconcile the two.

His political career falls into two periods: in the first, which lasted from 1831 to 1841, he was offered a minor post in Lord Melbourne's administration which he refused pleading the demands of literature; in the second, from 1852 to 1859 he accepted Lord Derby's offer of the Secretaryship of the Colonies. By then increasing deafness and the virulent attacks of Rosina had soured his appetite for Westminster. It was a long way from the heady days of 1831 when as the young member for St Ives he was swept into Parliament in the ferment surrounding the passage of the Reform Bill. He had been elected as a supporter of the Bill and on 5th July he made his maiden speech in its favour. St Ives was one of the constituencies which vanished after the Act received the Royal Assent in June 1832 and Bulwer selected in place of it the constituency of Lincoln which he represented until his resignation in 1841. Bulwer attended the House of Commons regularly and spoke occasionally, always with great effect. His second speech concerned the English theatre. This was a subject upon which he already felt deeply although the years of his personal connection with the stage were yet to come. Bulwer's speech, which was delivered in May 1832, called for a Select Committee to investigate the various anomalies which existed in English theatrical life: to abolish the monopoly on all serious dramatic

21

works which was held by the two patent theatres, Covent Garden and Drury Lane; to consider introducing dramatic copyright which did not exist at all; and to reconsider the question of censorship. On the last point Bulwer felt strongly. The public taste, he argued, backed by a vigilant press was the only civilised form of censorship. 'The true censor of the age', he told the Commons, 'is the spirit of the age.'

A fortnight later Bulwer brought forward a motion to reduce the tax levied on newspapers which he described as a tax on knowledge; cheap knowledge, he argued, was possibly a better political agent than costly punishment.

Bulwer's activities were not wholly directed to cultural measures; he occupied himself with Irish affairs and in promoting the reform of the Factory and the Poor Laws.

He was moderately busy during the 1834 session which terminated abruptly with the downfall of Lord Grey's Government in July. He made a short visit to Ireland, reporting in detail his impressions of the country to Disraeli who he had hoped would accompany him. It was in Ireland that Bulwer heard of the autumn crisis and the resignation of Lord Melbourne who had succeeded Grey in the summer. The fall of the government had been hastened by the death of Lord Spencer and the subsequent loss to the Commons of his son, Lord Althorp. The Duke of Wellington advised the King to summon Sir Robert Peel from Rome and ask him to form a government. Bulwer and his friends realised the importance of retaining Melbourne at the helm. He hurried home from Ireland and in two days he wrote the pamphlet *A Letter to a Late Cabinet Minister on the Present Crisis* which did more than anything else to secure a majority for the Whigs in the December election. Its passionate defence of the reform movement made it an instant best-seller, twenty-one editions were sold in six weeks and it provided the basis for most of the Whig speeches and addresses delivered before the election. The subsequent Whig majority was largely due to the influence of the pamphlet, and when Melbourne finally reassumed the premiership the offer to Bulwer of a minor government position reflected his gratitude.

DOUBTS AND WITHDRAWAL

Bulwer's refusal of office marked a turning point in his early

Left: 'A Pair', a contemporary cartoon of Bulwer and Disraeli (1839).

Below: the House of Commons in 1833, by George Hayter. Bulwer would be sitting among the Whigs on the left. From about 1831 Charles Dickens sat in the gallery reporting for the 'Mirror of Parliament'. One building was burned to the ground in 1834.

political life. He continued to attend and to take an active interest in all that occurred in the House but he was never completely at ease in the Whig Party. In 1835 he considered joining a small group of philosophical radicals to form a new party. On this point he sought the advice of his political mentor, Lord Durham. Bulwer's subsequent political career, had Lord Durham assumed high office, is a matter for speculation. They were close friends in private as well as being allies in public; in October 1834 a letter of Bulwer's to Lady Blessington refers to Lord Durham's premiership as a certainty. 'Durham', he wrote, 'has written his horoscope on the people's heart, and they only want the occasion to tell him of his destiny.' But this was not to be. It is difficult not to connect Bulwer's withdrawal from politics in 1841 with Lord Durham's death the previous year.

Bulwer's last speech in the House as a Liberal was his greatest oratorical triumph. It was delivered on 22nd May 1838 in support of a motion for the immediate abolition of the twelve-year apprenticeship of emancipated slaves which had followed the abolition of slavery in the British colonies. The scheme had failed and Bulwer added his plea for the resolution. 'We cannot demand compensation for the negro—we cannot call back the past. . . But justice and sympathy for the future—*these* at least are in our power!' O'Connell had intended to speak but words failed him, he tore up his notes and cried, 'The case is made out—there is nothing to add, divide.' The resolution was carried and the Lincoln papers reported with approbation that Mrs Bulwer-Lytton celebrated the emancipation of the negro apprentices by donating bread, meat and ale to the poor at Knebworth.

The stage

BULWER AND MACREADY

Bulwer's love for the stage was long-standing. 'That Fairy Land to the vision of the worldly', he wrote in *Zanoni,* and his efforts in parliament on the theatre's behalf were presented with the complete conviction that stems from personal involvement. Bulwer was in fact at that time in the midst of planning a dramatic trilogy based on the life of Oliver Cromwell. He had laid this aside and on his first meeting with the actor-manager Macready in Dublin in the autumn of 1834, he had to confess that part of the manuscript had been lost. From time to time the two, novelist and actor, met at parties in London but it was not until Macready received a summons to visit Bulwer in Albany in February 1836 that the subject of play-writing was renewed. It happened in dramatic fashion. Bulwer announced that he had written a play, that the principal part had been conceived with Macready in mind and that the published book would be dedicated to him. For two seasons Macready had been pounding the boards of Drury Lane in second-rate melodramas. Quite unexpectedly one of the most distinguished novelists of the day offers him a tailor-made play. He was overcome. Although the *Duchesse de la Vallière* did not provide a perfect vehicle for the display of Macready's powers when it was finally performed on 4th January 1837, it marked the beginning of a brief but brilliant partnership between actor and author and the subsequent creation of three immensely successful plays, *The Lady of Lyons* (1838), *Richelieu* (1839) and *Money* (1840).

La Vallière was in fact a complete failure. Bulwer was not dispirited; he learned much from the staging of the play, from the critics whose words he heeded for once, and from the reaction of the audience. When Macready pressed for another work, Bulwer produced *The Lady of Lyons.* Macready had by

25

Bulwer-Lytton

William Charles Macready, the actor-manager, about 1843, from an engraving of a miniature by Robert Thorburn. Bulwer said of Macready: 'He has identified himself with the living drama of his period, and by so doing he has half created it.'

this time taken over the management of Covent Garden and it was duly announced that on 15th February 1838 he would appear for the first time in a new play by an unknown author. It was not the first time that Bulwer had hidden behind the cloak of anonymity and it would not be the last. In the case of *The Lady of Lyons* he need not have worried—the play was a resounding success. The pit rose to cheer again and again and the reviews were excellent. Bulwer did not attend the first night as he was speaking in the House of Commons, but he hurried to the theatre as soon as he could to join Lady Blessington in her box. The review in the *Examiner* was particularly warm. 'It was a scene to raise, to revive, to give a new zest to play-going,' it ran; the author, John Forster, had become by this time one of Bulwer's closest friends, but even if he suspected that Bulwer had written the play he did not know officially until the secret was divulged. Forster was an important ally; by 1835 at the early age of twenty-one he had become the influential literary and dramatic critic of the *Examiner* and it was to Forster that both Macready and Bulwer turned for advice throughout the later years of their collaboration. *Richelieu,* Bulwer's next attempt at a drama, was read to him by Macready one night after dinner; by the fifth act Forster had fallen fast asleep, a lapse Bulwer found hard to forgive.

Richelieu is historical drama on the grand scale and the title-role displayed Macready's talents at their best. 'Magnificent

Opposite, top: farewell dinner to Macready, attended by over 600 friends and admirers. Bulwer is seated on his left.

Opposite, bottom: the piquet scene from 'Money', with Macready seated on the right.

26

costume, gorgeous decoration, splendid scenery,' commented *The Times*. Author and actor had worked in close collaboration from the start. By the opening night Macready's temper was at breaking point and he confided to his diary that Bulwer was not quite as *docile* as he had originally imagined him to be. But pique could not survive long in the face of *Richelieu's* success, and when Bulwer outlined plans for yet another play Macready's only comment was, 'What an indefatigable man!'

THE SUCCESS OF 'MONEY'

The writing of *Money,* which proved to be the last fruit of the Bulwer-Macready partnership, occupied Bulwer throughout the summer months of 1840. It was a respite. Rosina had renewed her attacks with redoubled energy and he was feeling old and tired and rather shaken. Both Macready and Forster were alarmed at his state of health and it was with some sense of relief that they packed him off to the continent with the sketch of the new play in hand. By the beginning of November they had progressed as far as discussing costumes; by the end of the month rehearsals had begun. All was far from smooth, Forster was critical and Bulwer so nervy that Macready had to mediate between him and the actors.

The first night finally took place on 8th December; the success was instantaneous and packed some eighty houses before the end of the season. Bulwer's choice of a modern comedy was a welcome change after the somewhat turgid rhetoric of his earlier efforts and revivals in this century have proved that its satire has stood the test of time. It was a sumptuous production. Walter Lacy, who played Sir Frederick Blount, recalled years later how Count D'Orsay's tailor had been brought in to advise on the men's costumes and how the complete change of costume for each of the five acts had absorbed the first five weeks of his salary.

Bulwer did not give up writing for the stage; he wrote a play for Charles Dickens *Not So Bad As We Seem,* and notes and references show that ideas for plays were constantly in his mind. His friendship with Macready survived the collaboration. At the farewell dinner to Macready in 1851 when six hundred friends and admirers joined together to mark his retirement from the stage, it was Edward Bulwer who spoke on behalf of them all.

The novels of middle life

WORK AT KNEBWORTH

The last years of the 1830s were sad ones for Bulwer despite his successes on the stage; Rosina had gone but she gave him no peace. 'I tremble every day,' he wrote in his diary in 1838, 'lest my domestic sores should be dragged still more into light, and all that is most sacred in men's hearths and homes exposed to all that is most galling in public gossip.' Yet there were compensations. He had made a name for himself in Parliament, as a novelist and as a writer for the theatre; he had received a baronetcy for his services to literature in the Coronation Honours List of 1838; he was surrounded by loyal friends. Lady Blessington remained a trusted confidante through all his sorrows. 'I cannot long be alone with the Past,' he wrote to her about this time, 'I must ever be busied with little anxieties created for myself, in order to escape from the terrible stillness within.' John Forster was always near at hand, for advice, for companionship. Disraeli had re-entered Bulwer's life as their political views grew closer. 'My dear E.L.B.,' he wrote in 1837, 'our friendship has stood many tests. If I analyse the causes I would ascribe them in some degree to a warm heart on my side and a generous temper on yours.' Much of literary London retained a deep affection for Bulwer. As editor of the *New Monthly* his generosity to writers in financial distress was well-known; Leigh Hunt, Laman Blanchard and Tom Hood were three who, at one stage or another of their lives, received his assistance.

In 1841 Bulwer resigned his seat as M.P. for Lincoln. The eleven years he remained out of Parliament saw the production of some of his most distinguished literary work accomplished between sporadic outbreaks of illness, mental strain and a restlessness which was soothed in some measure by travel.

In 1843 his mother died. 'In her I have lost a thousand ties in

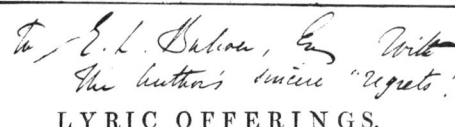

LYRIC OFFERINGS,

BY

LAMAN BLANCHARD.

" Our poesy is as a gum, which oozeth
" From whence 'tis nourished."
Timon of Athens.

LONDON:
WILLIAM HARRISON AINSWORTH.
OLD BOND STREET.
MDCCCXXVIII.

Above: Bulwer's book-plate.

Left: Title-page of Laman Blanchard's 'Lyric Offerings' published by Harrison Ainsworth in 1828 and much praised by Bulwer.

one,' he wrote, and memories of the bitter past were revived, of the quarrels, of the angry exchanges at the time of his marriage, and of his mother's subsequent affection, solicitude and understanding. He inherited Knebworth, he commissioned Kendall to rebuild and John Crace to redecorate, he ordered new curtains, new furniture, exotic wallpapers, and he redesigned the garden. After he had parted with 36 Hertford Street, Bulwer had never stayed long in any London house; Knebworth was now a refuge where he could write undisturbed,

Opposite: (top) Knebworth House, Bulwer's home in Hertfordshire, in 1847 after H.E.Kendall had embellished the house with turrets, domes and gargoyles; (bottom) Bulwer's library at Knebworth, showing the original decorations by John Grace.

C

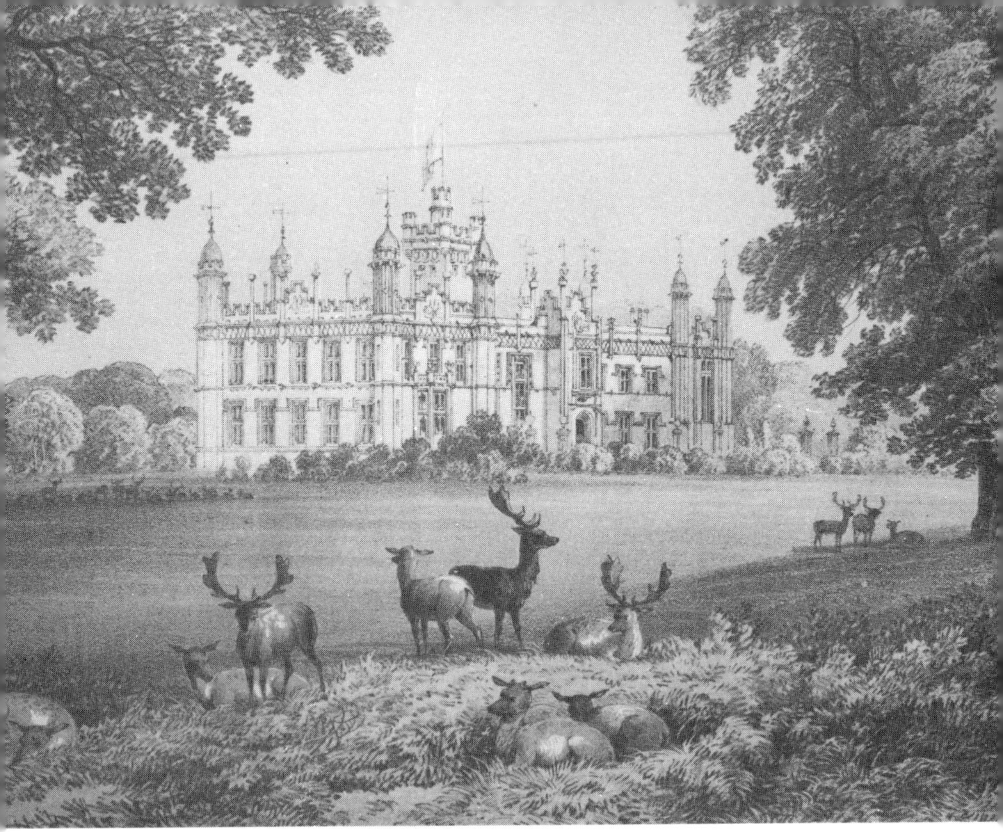

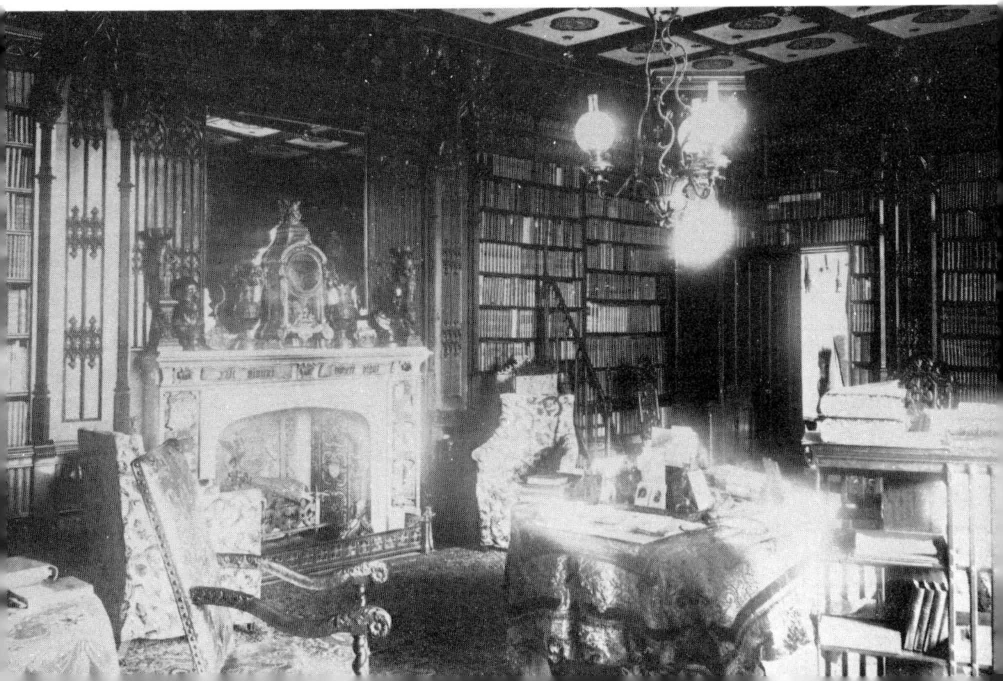

read, ride and entertain his friends. His clothes became simpler, the whiskers gradually disappeared and he grew a neat moustache. He slept no better, ate sparingly and smoked incessantly, seven cigars were laid out on the table by his bed and frequently all were gone by morning. Bulwer always maintained a London house but from now Knebworth came first in his affections and, to the end of his life, its embellishment was a constant source of delight.

At Knebworth Bulwer was able to indulge his passion for historical romance to the full. The Lyttons had inherited the house through marriage in 1492. The Banqueting Hall contained an elaborate Jacobean screen and pine panelling in the purest late-seventeenth-century Italianate style. Bulwer filled the room with suits of armour (two of which were given to him by Harrison Ainsworth), the standards the Lyttons had borne in battle from the fifteenth century onwards, and paintings of English kings; he bought a huge painting after Titian of the Emperor Charles V at Mühlberg, rich hangings from the Medici collections, tapestries, chairs and sofas covered in the crimson velvet and silver embroidery removed from James I's state bedroom at Wanstead. Bulwer, Kendall and Crace conjured out of the sedate shell that Mrs Bulwer-Lytton had bequeathed a fairy-tale palace with battlements, turrets, domes and gargoyles. Visitors gasped at the sight of Bulwer's fantasy set in the midst of the quiet Hertfordshire landscape.

In 1841 he published *Night and Morning* which followed *Paul Clifford* and *Eugene Aram* as the third of his novels in which crime is the theme. In this case the hero is not criminal, rather his friend and benefactor is, and once again the old charge of immorality was levelled at Bulwer. 'It is not immoral, it is moral,' he wrote to Forster, 'and of the most impressive and epic order of morals, to arouse and sustain interest for a criminal. It is immoral when you commend the crime, and this from the first page of *Pelham* to the last of *Night and Morning* I have never done.'

BULWER AND THE OCCULT

Bulwer's interest in occult studies stemmed from his Cambridge days and his passion for prediction and the casting of horoscopes was well known to his friends. It is said, but the evidence is quite inconclusive, that Bulwer was received as an adept in a Rosicrucian house in Frankfurt on one of his early travels on the continent. Kenneth Mackenzie, who knew Bulwer well and was a Rosicrucian himself, spoke of the latter as a neophyte, the first rung on the Rosicrucian ladder, and Bulwer was considered a suitable candidate for the office of Grand Patron of the Rosicrucian Society of England when it was founded in 1866. The secrecy surrounding the order and its adepts makes any confirmation of his precise status difficult to establish. He was not a Freemason as were his father and brother Henry, a factor which would have precluded ordinary membership of the Rosicrucian Society of England. But his status in occult circles in England was high and Eliphas Lévi, on his visit to London in 1854, regarded Bulwer as one of the principal exponents of occult studies in the country. This reputation was due in large measure to his Rosicrucian novel *Zanoni* which appeared in 1842.

Zanoni, an adept and the hero of the story, has, through the renunciation of all earthly ties, desires and affections and through intensive study and faith, attained spiritual perfection and the secret of eternal life. But his love for Viola, a beautiful Neapolitan singer, is his downfall. He breaks faith, but in dying for her he attains a greater happiness than he had known through all the ages of his existence. The book is steeped in Rosicrucian lore. The idea of Zanoni as a character had occurred to Bulwer in a dream in the mid 1830s when he was making extensive studies in the occult sciences. 'In dreams commences all human knowledge,' he was to write, 'in dreams hovers over measureless space the first faint bridge between spirit and spirit—this world and the world beyond.' *Zicci* was the first fruit of these investigations; this was an unfinished story which he contributed in 1838 to Harrison Ainsworth's *Monthly Chronicle,* and it was from *Zicci* that the finished story of *Zanoni* grew. It was Bulwer's favourite creation and contains some of the most beautiful prose he ever wrote.

THE LAST HISTORICAL NOVELS

His next novel *The Last of the Barons,* which appeared in 1843, was in strong contrast to *Zanoni.* Bulwer reverted to another of his abiding interests, the romance of the Middle Ages in general, and the Wars of the Roses in particular. His hero, Richard Neville, Earl of Warwick, the King-maker, the last representative of the old feudal Plantagenet world, and Edward IV, the representative of the new, provided an analogy with Bulwer's age which he exploited to the full. The clash between the two systems provided enough plots and counter-plots to make a story whose popularity proved enormous. Warwick himself Bulwer described as 'one of the few characters I have conceived that I take a personal affection for'. At the time he announced that it would probably be his last work of fiction; this was not in fact the case, but it did mark a respite in which Bulwer battled against ill-health, deep depression and the upheaval which followed his mother's death. He spent much time abroad. Rosina's taunts continued but the scandal surrounding the publication of her novel *Cheveley: or the Man of Honour* which lampooned Bulwer in the cruellest fashion, had largely died down.

It is all the more surprising that Bulwer should have dived into another hornets' nest and stirred up his old enemies, the Tory critics, by the publication of his long poem *The New Timon. The New Timon,* which described contemporary life in London, was published anonymously in 1845-6; its fame rests largely on the unfortunate and most unwarranted attack he made on Tennyson both as poet and as man. 'School-miss Alfred' was stirred to action, and whether it was he himself or John Forster who guessed the identity of the author of the offensive lines, the public were left in no doubt when Tennyson's reply was printed in *Punch*:

'I *thought* we knew him! What, it's you,—
The padded man that wears the stays!'

In 1846 he wrote from Rome to Lady Blessington, 'I long again to be in public life, though the old illusions are dispelled. However, let politics rest for the present.' He was writing again. *Lucretia,* the last of his crime novels, was published that year. *The Caxtons,* which he began about this time, one of his most delightful novels of contemporary life, full of acute observations, catching to perfection the spirit of the day, did not appear until 1849. In 1848 he had composed his most ambitious poetical work, *King Arthur,* and his last historical novel, *Harold,* which contains a vivid re-creation of the closing years of Edward the Confessor's reign and the establishment of the Norman dynasty under William I.

The decade ended with two crushing blows. In 1848 his

Above left: a rare photograph of Bulwer, taken c.1855.

Above right: Charles Dickens by Daniel Maclise in 1839, of which Thackeray wrote: 'As a likeness perfectly amazing'.

daughter Emily died after a severe attack of typhoid fever; she was followed a year later by Lady Blessington. Emily's death was the signal for a further outbreak of violent abuse between her parents. Bulwer, who had seen so little of her, was shattered by the news. 'She is dead,' he wrote to Forster, 'dead, Emily my child. Pity me! I am crushed down.' She was twenty. Lady

KNEBWORTH PRIVATE THEATRICALS.

On Monday, November 18th, will be performed

BEN JONSON'S COMEDY

OF

EVERY MAN IN HIS HUMOUR.

KNOWELL, *an Old Gentleman*	. MR. DELMÉ RADCLIFFE.
EDWARD KNOWELL, *his Son*	. MR. HENRY HAWKINS
BRAINWORM, *the Father's Man*	. MR. MARK LEMON.
GEORGE DOWNRIGHT, *a Plain Squire*	. MR. FRANK STONE.
WELLBRED, *his Half-brother*	. MR. HENRY HALE.
KITELY, *a Merchant*	. MR. JOHN FORSTER.
CAPTAIN BOBADIL, *a Paul's Man*	. MR. CHARLES DICKENS.
MASTER STEPHEN, *a Country Gull*	. MR. DOUGLAS JERROLD.
MASTER MATHEW, *the Town Gull*	. MR. JOHN LEECH.
THOMAS CASH, *Kitely's Cashier*	. MR. FREDERICK DICKENS.
OLIVER COB, *a Water-bearer*	. MR. AUGUSTUS EGG.
JUSTICE CLEMENT, *an old merry Mavistrcte*	. THE HON. ELIOT YORKE, M.P.
ROGER FORMAL, *his Clerk*	. MR. PHANTOM.
DAME KITELY, *Kitely's Wife*	. MISS MARY BOYLE.
MISTRESS BRIDGET, *his Sister*	. MISS HOGARTH.
TIB, *Cob's Wife*	. MRS. CHARLES DICKENS.

THE EPILOGUE BY MR. DELMÉ RADCLIFFE.

To conclude with MRS. INCHBALD'S *Farce of*

ANIMAL MAGNETISM.

THE DOCTOR	. MR. CHARLES DICKENS.
LA FLEUR	. MR. MARK LEMON.
THE MARQUESS DE LANCY	. MR. JOHN LEECH.
JEFFREY	. MR. AUGUSTUS EGG.
CONSTANCE	. MISS HOGARTH.
LISETTE	. MISS MARY BOYLE.

*Stage Manager—*MR. CHARLES DICKENS.

The Theatre will be open at half-past Six. The Performance will begin precisely at

HALF-PAST SEVEN.

The cast list of 'Every Man in His Humour' and 'Animal Magnetism', as performed by Dickens and others at Knebworth in 1850.

36

Blessington's death marked the end of an era. She was Bulwer's closest friend, his confidante and his support at every crisis. Her going left a void which would never be filled; to Bulwer she was as Ione in the *Last Days of Pompeii,* 'one of those brilliant characters which, but once or twice, flash across our career'.

The greater part of 1849 was spent abroad and it was not until June 1850 that Bulwer returned to Knebworth.

DICKENS AND THE GUILD OF LITERATURE

The year 1850 saw the publication of *David Copperfield.* For the previous thirteen years, from the appearance of *Pickwick Papers* in 1837, Dickens's reputation had been steadily growing until by the middle of the century he had eclipsed all rivals. Bulwer and Dickens had met at Harrison Ainsworth's in the late 1830s and had quickly become friends. In November 1850, Dickens, at Bulwer's suggestion, brought his amateur theatrical company to perform at Knebworth. The company was star-studded. It included Dickens himself, Douglas Jerrold, Mark Lemon, John Forster, John Leech and Augustus Egg. The play selected was Ben Jonson's *Every Man in His Humour* which they performed in the Banqueting Hall for three nights with a different farce each night as a finale. 'Everything', Dickens wrote, 'has gone off in a whirl of triumph, and fired the whole length and breadth of the county of Hertfordshire.'

It was during the theatricals at Knebworth that Dickens and Bulwer evolved the idea of mounting further performances to raise money to establish a guild to benefit impoverished authors and artists. The tragic death of Laman Blanchard in 1845 in dire poverty moved Bulwer deeply; as long ago as 1828 he had received as Editor of the *New Monthly Magazine* Blanchard's *Lyric Offerings,* one of the few books published by Harrison Ainsworth. Bulwer reviewed the slim volume with lavish praise. But Blanchard did not survive the perils and uncertainties of a life devoted to literature and it was with such men in mind that Bulwer and Dickens thought out their scheme. 'There is a great power that has grown up about you,' Bulwer wrote to Dickens, 'out of a winter night's amusement, and do let us try and use it for the lasting service of our order.' A plan of campaign was drawn up. Bulwer was to write a comedy for Dickens and his troupe to perform. He set to work. Before long he had produced a comedy which delighted Dickens, who promptly entitled it *Not So Bad As We Seem*. Dickens could hardly wait to start rehearsals. 'We are all agog here, standing like greyhounds (especially Lemon, who is very like a greyhound) in the slips.' Their chance came. The Duke of Devonshire proved a delightfully willing patron and accordingly on 16th May 1851 the comedy was enacted before the Queen, Prince Albert and a fashionable audience at Devonshire House. The evening was a resounding success, the Queen donated £100 and at the supper which followed she sat on a throne which Richard Hengist Horne described as 'surmounted by a Gothic arch, elaborately decorated with roses, magnolias, jasmine and honeysuckle'.

A triumphal tour of the provinces followed which ended with a public dinner in Manchester at which both Bulwer and Dickens explained their scheme in detail. Slowly the funds appeared, £4,000 in all, and in 1854 Bulwer carried a bill through Parliament to incorporate the Guild of Literature and Art. The expressed purpose of the Guild was to assist members financially by the provision of pensions, to obtain adequate insurance, to establish a Provident Sickness Fund and to provide rent-free accommodation for those who wanted it. The idea of a brotherhood of artists and authors underlay the more practical considerations and in 1863 Bulwer made a free gift of land on his estate for the Guild Houses. It was a splendid idea but it failed, not for lack of money or enthusiasm but for lack of support from those it was intended to benefit.

In 1860 Dickens asked Bulwer to write a story to appear in serial form in his magazine *All the Year Round*. *A Strange Story* appealed enormously to Dickens. He wrote to Bulwer, 'I received your revised proofs. . . I *could not* lay them aside, but was obliged to go on with them in my bedroom until I got into a very ghostly state indeed.' The story was a return to the mysticism of *Zanoni*, and again the theme occurred to Bulwer in a dream. But the spell it cast over Dickens did not have the same effect on the public and the story was unfavourably received by the critics.

Bulwer greatly enjoyed the company of Dickens, who made a second visit to Knebworth in 1861 bringing with him the proofs of *Great Expectations* for Bulwer's comments. His friend, Dickens thought, was 'in better health and spirits than I have seen him in all these years. . . brilliantly talkative, anecdotal, and droll'.

The Devonshire House performance of 'Not So Bad As We Seem', before Queen Victoria and Prince Albert, from the 'Illustrated London News', 24th May 1851.

The Institute of the Guild of Literature and Art at Stevenage, founded by Charles Dickens and Bulwer, from the 'Illustrated London News', 12th August 1865.

Secretary of State for the Colonies

TORY MEMBER FOR HERTFORDSHIRE

The Corn Laws were the backcloth against which English politics raged during the eleven years Bulwer was in the political wilderness. He himself was strongly against a repeal of the Corn Laws, a view which was also shared by the majority of the Tory party. Sir Robert Peel's sudden conversion to the policy of Free Trade in 1846 appalled Bulwer, infuriated the other Protectionists, and brought about the fall of Peel's administration. Bulwer had great respect for Lord John Russell who followed Peel, but Russell's term of office increased Bulwer's general sense of disillusion with the Whigs.

But Bulwer's appetite for politics had been whetted once more. He stood very little chance of entering Parliament as a Liberal unless he abandoned his Protectionist sympathies; the only alternative lay with the Tory party. Politics in England had changed greatly since the 1830s. Bulwer remained a reformer at heart but he had watched with ill-concealed distaste the gradual domination of his party by the commercial interests of the industrial Midlands. It was at this time that his friendship with Disraeli led him to look again at certain elements within the Tory party which had no counterparts within the old Tory party of the 1830s. A weekend visit by Disraeli and his wife to Knebworth in 1851, when the two men talked politics ceaselessly, set the seal on Bulwer's conversion. His *Letters to John Bull* published in 1851, which neatly defined the Protectionist standpoint, was praised by Disraeli and led to the electors of Hertfordshire inviting Bulwer to become their Member. In the General Election of 1852 Bulwer was duly elected and he continued to represent that constituency in Parliament in the Tory interest until he was given a peerage in 1866.

When Parliament met, the Tories headed by Lord Derby were

in office but in the minority and by the end of the year they were in opposition. Bulwer played a small part but his health was precarious and for a short period in 1853 he lost the use of his right hand. 'I am not at all up to Parliament,' he wrote to his son, 'and to add to my misfortunes am so deaf as not to hear the speaker.'

But the events leading up to the Crimean War and the effect of the war on the country as it ran its disastrous course saw Bulwer once more in the forefront of the House and he spoke frequently and with great effect.

'Oh, to be a raw recruit of 18, setting off for the dismal swamp of the Crimea,' he wrote to Forster in January 1855, 'full of hope, dreamless of sciatica and pining for a word in a despatch... But that army, what a state! How one's heart bleeds! What blame attaches somewhere. Is it Raglan really?'

It was widely expected that Lord Derby would form an administration when Lord Aberdeen was forced to resign in the face of mounting criticism on the conduct of the war. But he refused. Bulwer, whose Parliamentary reputation stood high after his interventions, would almost certainly have been offered a place in his administration.

Literary work continued spasmodically. His last melodramatic novel *My Novel,* which contains an interesting picture of English political life at the beginning of the nineteenth century, was published in 1853 and he amused himself with translations from the Classics. *What Will He Do With It?* was published in *Blackwood's Magazine* in serial form. In February 1858, just as he had dispatched the last chapter to the publishers, Lord Palmerston's government was defeated. Lord Derby replaced him and in May Bulwer found himself Secretary of State for the Colonies.

BRITISH COLUMBIA

Bulwer's period of office was short but not without interest. It began tragically and inauspiciously with the appearance of Rosina shouting abuse at him in Hertford at the election which followed his appointment as minister. Her mind appeared at times totally unhinged but she was far from being insane and the steps Bulwer took at this time to have her declared so were most unwise. Rosina threatened to collect a crowd outside the Colonial Office to denounce her husband, the Press took up her case and pressed for a public enquiry. Bulwer's ministerial colleagues were alarmed. At this point Robert, their son, came to the rescue. Rosina was released, Bulwer increased her allowance, always a bone of contention between them, and mother and son left for some uneasy weeks on the continent. Bulwer was shaken to the core; there was no knowing when Rosina would appear again or which of his colleagues would be the recipient of one of her venomous missives. Depression descended on him again, but he had his work and this he greatly enjoyed.

The most important act of his period in office was the incorporation of British Columbia as a new colony. Vancouver Island had been placed under the jurisdiction of the Hudson's Bay Company in 1849: the mainland was then the haunt of trappers and Indians. The discovery of gold on the banks of the Fraser River brought a flood of immigration and the necessity for urgent action by the Government to establish some form of administrative control. Bulwer's high hopes and expectations for the future are the kernel of his speeches on the subject and he always maintained his interest in the thriving colony.

He also presided over the separation of Queensland from New South Wales and he made the appointment of the governor of the new colony a matter of minute concern.

RESIGNATION AND A PEERAGE

By the end of 1858 Bulwer's health had completely broken down once more; he longed to resign but Derby and Disraeli pleaded with him to remain. For the good of the administration he lingered on but in May 1859 his release came. He remained in Parliament until 1866, but he never held office again, although he occasionally intervened on the subject of parliamentary reform.

In 1866 Lord Derby offered Bulwer a peerage; he accepted it gratefully. For generations the Lyttons had distinguished themselves in public life but the family had never been ennobled. He chose the title Baron Lytton of Knebworth. 'Do you remember the evening when you and I were riding together,' he wrote to Robert, 'and I said "We must have the Peerage. I can but be a Baron—higher grades I leave to you"?'

Bulwer took his seat in the House of Lords but he did not speak. He could hear nothing in the vast chamber. 'I sat next a

Seven great Indian chiefs in attendance on the Governor of British Columbia, c.1860. From an album of views of British Columbia presented to Bulwer-Lytton.

man who seemed trying his best to hear Derby, whose voice is the most audible, and I said to him—"Do you hear?" "Only a word or two here and there," was the encouraging answer.'

It is possible that he might have held office again. His health did return and with it the rekindling of his Parliamentary ambitions. But it was too late. In 1864 he received a shattering blow. Disraeli told him Rosina had renewed her attacks. 'This horrible calamity weighs on me, but I know not what to do. . . But the thing effectively damps the ardour I was beginning to have for politics.' Robert, his son, understood and sympathised but there was nothing he could do. The journey he had undertaken with his mother at the height of the last crisis had ended in a total breach. From that moment Rosina's fury was vented on both father and son. Neither was to meet her again.

Last days

FAREWELL TO DICKENS

The last years of Bulwer's life were restless. He wandered from place to place, to spas, to health-cures, to Nice, he even revisited Naples, but ill-health and depression dogged his footsteps. The loneliness of his life had largely been banished by reading and by intense literary activity. This increasingly became a burden. He was still a copious letter writer and the long letters to and from his son Robert, whose diplomatic career entailed long absences abroad, were among the great joys of his old age.

One of the last glimpses of Bulwer at a public gathering was in 1867, appropriately enough at the farewell banquet given to Dickens before his second and last visit to the United States. Five hundred people assembled to watch Dickens, in failing health, enter the hall on Bulwer's arm. Bulwer was in the chair; his speech was interrupted again and again by cheers. When Dickens rose to speak, the assembly went wild, men jumped on chairs, throwing their napkins in the air, waving glasses and decanters over their heads. Dickens stood and watched, the tears streaming down his face, waiting to speak. Three years later he was dead; few of Bulwer's friends survived him. The passage of time and regret for the past are themes that recur again and again in Bulwer's writings. Finally he came to terms with both. 'If we cannot stop time,' he once wrote, 'it is something to shoe him with felt, and prevent his steps from creaking.' Intermittently he worked as hard as he had as a young man. He kept closely in touch with the world of literature and politics and towards the end of the 1860s he saw much of Lady Sherborne, who coaxed him once more into London life.

THE COMING RACE

Bulwer was at work almost to the end. *The Coming Race,* a

Bulwer in his study, by E.M.Ward, 1854.

remarkable and strangely prophetic feat of imagination, was published in 1871. The hero, a young American, falls down the shaft of a mine and finds himself in an underground world inhabited by a people, the Vrilya, whose knowledge and habits had progressed far beyond anything known to the world on earth. It was a satire, for the Vrilya were a utopian community with each of the virtues of their philosophy realised to its fullest extent. Bulwer referred to the book as a 'quiz on Darwin and Radical politics'. It was an enormous success.

Kenelm Chillingly was finished a few days before his death. His letters he left carefully arranged in albums with the generous comments on his friends neatly written in the margins. Caroline Lamb, Lord Durham, Thomas Talfourd, John Stuart Mill, Harrison Ainsworth, Thomas Campbell—virtually every distinguished figure of liberal sympathy in the world of public life, of literature, drama or art had been his friend or correspondent. His mind was active to the last; thirty years before, H.F.Chorley had written, 'It is a fine, energetic, inquisitive, romantic mind which if I mistake not has been blighted and opened too soon. There wants the repose—the peace.'

Bulwer died at Torquay on 18th January 1873 and was buried in Westminster Abbey.

THE PRINCIPAL EVENTS OF
EDWARD BULWER-LYTTON'S LIFE

1803   Edward George Earle Lytton Bulwer born
1822   Fellow Commoner of Trinity Hall, Cambridge
1824-6 Travel in England and abroad
1827   Marries Rosina Doyle Wheeler
1828   *Pelham* and *The Disowned*
1829   *Devereux*
1830   *Paul Clifford*
1831   Became Editor of the *New Monthly Magazine* and M.P. for St Ives, Huntingdonshire
1832   *Eugene Aram*. M.P. for Lincoln
1833   *Godolphin.* Breakdown of health and journey to Italy
1834   *The Last Days of Pompeii* and *Letter to a Late Cabinet Minister.* Met actor-manager Macready
1835   *Rienzi*
1836   Final separation from Rosina
1837   *The Duchesse de la Vallière* (first play) and *Ernest Maltravers*
1838   *The Lady of Lyons.* Created a baronet
1840   *Money*
1841   *Night and Morning.* Resigned seat in House of Commons
1842   *Zanoni*
1843   *The Last of the Barons*
1846   *Lucretia*
1848   *Harold* and *King Arthur*
1849   *The Caxtons*
1851   Joined Conservative Party
1852   M.P. for Hertford
1858   *What Will He Do With It?* Secretary of State for the Colonies
1861   *A Strange Story*
1866   Raised to the peerage as Lord Lytton of Knebworth.
1871   *The Coming Race*
1873   *Kenelm Chillingly.* Lord Lytton died on 18th January

Knebworth House as it is today.

BIBLIOGRAPHY
Apart from the novelist's own works, the most important sources are:

The Life of Edward Bulwer, First Lord Lytton by his grandson, the Earl of Lytton. 2 volumes. (London: Macmillan) 1913. The standard biography.

The Life, Letters and Literary Remains of Edward Bulwer, Lord Lytton by his son. 2 volumes. (London: Kegan Paul) 1883. An account of Bulwer's life to 1831.

Bulwer: A Panorama. Edward and Rosina 1803-1836 by Michael Sadleir. (London: Constable) 1931.

* * * * *

New Cambridge Bibliography of English Literature edited by George Watson, Volume III, pages 917-921 (Cambridge 1969). This contains a list of Bulwer's works and a full account of books and articles concerning him.

Catalogue of the Bulwer-Lytton Centenary Exhibition held at Knebworth House 1973.

Forthcoming
The writer of this volume is engaged in a full-length biography of Edward Bulwer-Lytton.

47

INDEX

Page numbers in italic refer to illustrations